RUNNING WITH MY HEART

Running With My Heart

ECHOES OF SARAH

David Olubiyi

Dabim Support Services Inc

Contents

Dedication		vii
Acknowledgement		ix
Foreword		xi
1	Introduction of Protagonist	1
2	Meeting Sarah	6
3	Getting to Know Each Other	11
4	Sarah's Dream	15
5	Discovering A Shared Love Of Music	18
6	Hesitation To Commit	21
7	Friends' Teasing	23
8	Sarah's Faith	25
9	Parents' disapproval	28
10	Falling Out	31
11	Making Amends	34
12	Reunited	37
13	Pursuing Sarah's Music Dreams	39
14	Parents' Disapproval Of Sarah's Music	41
15	Reconciling Dreams And Expectations	43

16	Caleb's Injury And Identity Crisis	46
17	Sarah's Illness	49
18	Caregiving And Sacrifice	52
19	Marriage	56
20	Declining Health	58
21	Sarah's Passing	60
22	Turning To Sarah's Music	63
23	Pursuing Music Career	66
24	Success in music	68
25	Reflection and remembrance	70

Epilogue 73

To all those who have experienced loss and found comfort in creativity, this book is dedicated to you. May the story of Caleb and Sarah inspire you to find hope and healing in the power of music.

Copyright © 2023 David Olubiyi.
All rights reserved. No part of this book may be reproduced or transmitted in any form or by any means, electronic or mechanical, including photocopying, recording or by any information storage and retrieval system, without permission in writing from the publisher.

Acknowledgement

I would like to express my heartfelt gratitude to all those who have supported me throughout this journey of writing this book.

First and foremost, I want to thank my family for their unwavering love, encouragement, and support. Their belief in me has been the driving force behind my writing, and I could not have done it without them.

I am also deeply grateful to my friends and colleagues who have offered their valuable insights and feedback on the manuscript, and who have been there to cheer me on through the highs and lows of the writing process.

To my editor and publishing team, thank you for your guidance and expertise in bringing this book to life.

And finally, to my readers, thank you for giving me the opportunity to share my story with you. I hope that this book touches your heart and inspires you to find healing and purpose in your own life.

Foreword

As I read the manuscript for this book, I was struck by the raw emotion and honesty in its pages. The author has poured their heart and soul into this story, and the result is a beautiful tribute to the power of love, music, and the human spirit.

Through the character of Caleb, we see the journey of grief and loss, and the struggle to find purpose and meaning in life. But we also see the transformative power of creativity, and the way that music can heal and inspire us in our darkest moments.

This book is a testament to the resilience of the human spirit, and a reminder that even in the face of tragedy, there is always hope. I am honored to have the opportunity to share this powerful and inspiring story with readers, and I know that it will touch the hearts of all who read it.

1

Introduction of Protagonist

* * *

Introduction of protagonist, high school senior named Caleb, who is a popular athlete but lacks direction in life.

* * *

Caleb strolled through the bustling campus, watching his fellow students hurry off to their classes. They all seemed to have a sense of direction, a purpose that they were striving towards. He couldn't help but feel envious as he observed them.

He stopped by a bench near the library and sat down, mulling over his own life. He had always been more interested in sports and hanging out with his friends than in academics. But now, as he looked around, he wondered if he had made the right choice.

"Hey man, what's up?" A voice interrupted his thoughts. It was his friend, Jeremy.

"Nothing much, just thinking about stuff," Caleb replied.

"What stuff?"

"Life stuff, you know? What am I doing here? What's my purpose?"

Jeremy looked at him quizzically. "What do you mean? You're here to get a degree and have fun."

"But is that enough? I mean, everyone else seems to have it all figured out. They know what they want to do and where they're going. I feel like I'm just drifting along without any real direction."

Jeremy leaned back, considering Caleb's words. "Well, what do you want to do?"

Caleb shrugged. "I don't know. That's the problem. I've never really thought about it."

Jeremy chuckled. "Well, maybe it's time you did. What are you interested in?"

Caleb thought for a moment. "I like sports. Maybe I could do something with that?"

"Like what?"

"I don't know, maybe be a coach or a trainer or something."

"Okay, so you've got a starting point. Now you just need to figure out how to get there. Talk to some people in that field, do some research, and see what steps you need to take."

Caleb nodded, feeling a little more hopeful. Maybe he didn't have it all figured out yet, but at least he had a starting point. He stood up and clasped Jeremy's hand.

"Thanks man, you always know what to say."

Jeremy grinned. "That's what friends are for. Now go out there and make a plan!"

Caleb walked through the crowded hallway towards his locker, his mind racing with a flurry of thoughts. For the first time in his life, he was questioning his choices and wondering if there was more to life than just sports.

As he spun the combination on his locker, his mind was consumed with doubts and uncertainties. Did he really want to spend the rest of his life on the field, chasing a ball around? Was there something more meaningful and fulfilling out there that he was meant to do?

He leaned against the locker, lost in thought, as a flurry of self-doubt began to consume him. He knew he had always been more interested in sports than academics, but now he was starting to realize that there was more to life than just games.

As he gazed out into the sea of students rushing past him, he couldn't help but feel a twinge of envy. They all seemed so driven and focused, like they had a clear purpose in life. Caleb, on the other hand, felt lost and adrift, with no real sense of direction.

He sighed deeply, trying to shake off the cloud of uncertainty that had descended upon him. He knew he needed to start thinking about his future and figuring out what he really wanted to do with his life. But where should he start? How could he even begin to figure it all out?

As he closed his locker and turned to head to his next class, he knew one thing for sure: he couldn't keep ignoring these questions and hoping that they would just go away. It was time to start exploring his options and discovering what path he was truly meant to follow

Caleb knew that he couldn't continue to go through the motions and pretend that everything was okay. He needed to make a change, to find his passion and figure out what he truly wanted to do with his life. The thought of it all was daunting, but he was determined to find his way.

He had always been content with his life before, content with playing sports and hanging out with his friends. But now, as he watched his fellow students hustle to their classes with a sense of purpose, he realized that he was missing something.

The thought of spending the rest of his life just going through the motions and settling for mediocrity filled him with a sense of dread. He knew that he was meant for something more, something greater than what he was currently doing.

But where should he start? How could he possibly find his passion and purpose in life? These were the questions that consumed his thoughts as he walked to his next class.

Caleb knew that this journey would not be easy. It would require him to step out of his comfort zone, to explore new things and take risks. It would be a journey of self-discovery, filled with ups and downs, successes and failures.

But he was determined to find his way. He was determined to discover what made him truly happy, what set his soul on fire. He was ready to put in the hard work, to make the sacrifices necessary to find his true calling.

Caleb was feeling lost and uncertain about his direction in life as he watched his fellow students rushing to their classes with a clear sense of purpose. He had never been interested in academics or studying, and had instead focused on sports and socializing with his friends. However, in that moment, Caleb began to feel envious of his peers and their drive to achieve their goals. He realized that he lacked direction and a clear purpose in life, which left him feeling adrift and uncertain about his future. This realization may have prompted him to reflect on his priorities and consider what steps he could take to find his own path and purpose in life.

Caleb walked into his first class of the day, English Literature, and scanned the room for a familiar face. Amidst the sea of unfamiliar faces, his eyes landed on a quiet girl with long brown hair and a book in her hands. He had seen her around before, but had never really paid her much attention. There was something about her that caught his eye today.

As the class began, Caleb found himself struggling to focus on the lecture. His eyes kept wandering towards the girl who was now taking notes furiously. He couldn't help but wonder what it would be like to be so focused and passionate about something like she seemed to be. Caleb had always been a jack of all trades and a master of none. He envied her dedication.

The girl seemed oblivious to Caleb's stares, engrossed in her work. He wondered what book she was reading that was so captivating. Caleb had always been more interested in sports and music than reading. However, something about this girl and her love for books intrigued him. He made a mental note to strike up a conversation with her after class.

As the bell rang, signaling the end of class, Caleb gathered his things and made his way towards the door. He couldn't help but notice the girl who sat next to him, who was still engrossed in her book. The cover of the book caught his eye - "To Kill a Mockingbird". Caleb had read that book before, but he had never really thought much of it. He wondered what it was about the book that had captured her attention.

As he stepped out into the hallway, Caleb felt a sense of restlessness wash over him. He had been feeling lost lately, like he was drifting without a clear direction. He knew he needed to find a purpose, but he had no idea where to start. He felt like he was standing at a crossroads, unsure which path to take.

Little did he know, that chance encounter with the girl in English Literature would set him on a path he never could have imagined. As he walked towards his next class, he couldn't help but think about the girl and the book she was reading. He wondered what it was about the book that had captured her attention and made her so passionate about literature.

2

Meeting Sarah

***

Caleb meets the shy, bookish, and deeply religious Sarah in their high school English class.

***

Caleb's curiosity about the quiet girl with the long brown hair, whom he had met in his English Literature class, only grew over the next few days. He had learned her name was Sarah, and he couldn't help but think about her. He was intrigued by her quiet and reserved demeanor, and he wanted to get to know her better.

Caleb observed that Sarah was always carrying a book with her, and he wondered what type of books she was interested in. He knew from their conversation in class that she was deeply religious, but he didn't know much else about her. He found himself wanting to strike up another conversation with her and learn more.

As the days went by, Caleb found himself going out of his way to run into Sarah. He would linger outside of their classroom after class, hoping to bump into her. Whenever he did, they would exchange small talk, and he found her to be sweet and kind.

Caleb was also surprised to discover that they had some things in common. While Sarah was deeply religious, Caleb had always been interested in spirituality and philosophy. He found that they could have meaningful conversations about these topics, and he enjoyed hearing her perspective.

Despite their differences, Caleb found that he was drawn to Sarah's intelligence, kindness, and passion for reading. He couldn't wait to get to know her better and learn more about her. As he walked home from school, he thought about what he could do to get closer to her, and he knew that he had found someone special.

As Caleb was leaving class, he spotted the quiet girl from his English Literature class sitting alone in the library, surrounded by books. He took a deep breath and approached her, introducing himself and striking up a conversation about what she was reading.

"Hey, I'm Caleb. Mind if I sit with you?" he asked, gesturing to the empty seat across from her.

The girl looked up and gave him a small smile. "Sure, I'm Emily," she replied, motioning for him to sit down.

Caleb noticed that she had a stack of books in front of her and asked, "Wow, that's a lot of books. What are you reading?"

Emily's eyes lit up, and she began telling Caleb about the different books she was reading, from classic literature to modern-day fiction. Caleb listened intently, amazed by her passion for reading.

To Caleb's surprise, the quiet girl with the long brown hair, Sarah, was warm and engaging. After class, they struck up a conversation about the book she was reading, and to Caleb's delight, Sarah was eager to share her thoughts about the books she loved. They talked about the characters, the themes, and the symbolism, and Caleb found himself drawn to her intelligence and her passion for learning.

As they walked to their next class, Sarah told Caleb about her favorite authors and the books that had impacted her the most. Caleb listened intently, fascinated by her insights and her articulate way of expressing herself. He realized that he had found someone who could help him expand his horizons and deepen his understanding of the world around him.

Over the next few weeks, Caleb and Sarah became fast friends. They met for coffee after class, discussing everything from literature to philosophy to current events. Caleb found himself looking forward to their conversations, eager to hear Sarah's thoughts and opinions on various topics.

One day, as they sat in a coffee shop, Sarah asked Caleb about his interests. Caleb hesitated for a moment, unsure of how to answer. He had always been interested in sports and music, but those seemed like trivial pursuits compared to Sarah's love of literature and learning. However, Sarah was genuinely interested in what he had to say, and Caleb found himself opening up to her.

As the weeks went by, Caleb and Sarah's friendship grew stronger. They began to spend more time together, studying after school and attending various school events. Their conversations became longer and more frequent, often lasting late into the night.

Another time, Caleb confided in Sarah about his struggles with time management. He told her about how he often got distracted and struggled to stay focused. Sarah shared some of her own study tips and suggested different techniques that might help Caleb stay on track. Caleb was grateful for Sarah's advice and made a conscious effort to implement some of her strategies.

On one occasion, Sarah shared with Caleb her passion for poetry. She recited one of her favorite poems and explained the meaning behind it. Caleb had never really been interested in poetry before, but Sarah's enthusiasm was infectious. He found himself drawn to the beauty of the words and the emotions they conveyed.

Caleb was surprised by how much he enjoyed spending time with Sarah. He had initially been drawn to her in their English Literature class due to her dedication to learning, but it was her quiet strength that kept him coming back. As they spent more time together, he found himself opening up to her in a way he never had before.

One day, as they sat together in the campus café, Caleb couldn't help but ask Sarah about her introverted nature. "I've always been drawn to outgoing people," he admitted, "but there's something about your quiet strength that intrigues me. How do you do it?" Sarah smiled softly and explained that while she enjoyed socializing, she found solace in quiet moments of reflection and introspection. Caleb found himself nodding in agreement, realizing that he too craved moments of stillness amidst the chaos of everyday life.

As the semester went on, Caleb and Sarah's conversations grew deeper and more personal. They discussed everything from their childhoods to their hopes and dreams for the future. Caleb found himself opening up to Sarah in a way he never had with anyone else. He realized that her quiet demeanor was not a barrier to connection, but rather an invitation to deeper understanding.

One evening, as they walked through the campus gardens, Sarah shared with Caleb her love for photography. She pulled out her camera and showed him some of her favorite shots, explaining how she used photography as a way to capture and share moments of beauty in the world. Caleb found himself captivated by the way she saw the world through her lens, and he realized that there was so much more to Sarah than he had initially assumed.

As their friendship deepened, Caleb found himself struggling with feelings he had never experienced before. He couldn't shake the sense that he was falling in love with Sarah, but he was hesitant to act on those feelings. He had always been a popular athlete, and he worried about what his friends and classmates would think if he started dating the shy, bookish girl from English class.

Caleb had always been skeptical of faith and kindness. He had grown up in a world that valued success and material wealth over anything else. However, when he met Sarah, everything changed.

Sarah had a quiet strength that drew Caleb to her. She never wavered in her faith, even when life threw obstacles in her way. Her kindness towards others was unwavering, and she never seemed to ask for anything in return.

As Caleb spent more time with Sarah, he began to see her in a new light. He realized that her faith and kindness were not weaknesses but strengths. He saw how they brought joy to others' lives and how they gave Sarah a sense of purpose.

Through Sarah, Caleb discovered a new way of living. He saw the value of living with purpose and integrity, and he wanted to be a better person. He began to re-evaluate his priorities and to think about what truly mattered in life

Little did he know, Sarah would be the one to help him find that purpose.

3

Getting to Know Each Other

* * *

Caleb is initially dismissive of Sarah, but they are paired up for a class project and start to get to know each other better.

* * *

Caleb found himself spending more and more time with Sarah as the school year progressed. They shared a few classes together, and whenever they had group projects, their teachers seemed to pair them up automatically.

Despite being paired up by their teachers, Caleb didn't mind working with Sarah. In fact, he enjoyed spending time with her. They had similar interests and often found themselves lost in conversation outside of class.

As they spent more time together, Caleb began to realize that he was developing feelings for Sarah. He didn't know if she felt the same way, but he couldn't help but hope that she did.

At first, Caleb had a dismissive attitude towards Sarah. He viewed her as a shy and religious girl, who didn't have much to offer beyond her books and faith. For him, spending time with friends and playing sports was more important than getting to know someone like Sarah.

However, as they began working on their class project together, Caleb's perception of Sarah began to shift. He noticed how intelligent and considerate she was. He began to realize that she had a unique perspective on things that he had never thought about before.

As they continued to work together, Caleb found himself increasingly drawn to Sarah's personality and character. He appreciated her ability to think deeply about issues and her willingness to challenge his own views. Gradually, Caleb began to see Sarah as someone he could learn from and respect.

Through their collaboration, Caleb and Sarah developed a deep friendship that extended beyond the classroom. Caleb came to appreciate Sarah's qualities and her beliefs, and he learned to value her as a person in her own right. By looking beyond his initial assumptions about her, Caleb discovered a whole new dimension to Sarah that he had never seen before.

As Caleb and Sarah spent more time together, Caleb began to feel more comfortable with opening up to her. He confided in her about the difficulties he was facing in his life, including his struggles with finding direction and living up to others' expectations.

To his surprise, Sarah was a great listener who listened to him with empathy and understanding. She didn't judge him or try to tell him what to do. Instead, she offered him her support and encouragement, telling him that he had the potential to be whoever he wanted to be. Caleb felt grateful for her kindness and appreciated her words of wisdom.

Sarah's support and encouragement helped Caleb gain more confidence in himself. He began to believe that he had the ability to make his own choices and follow his own dreams, regardless of what others might think. Caleb's conversations with Sarah helped him to see that there was more to life than just following the expectations of others.

Over time, Caleb began to see Sarah as a trusted confidant and friend. He realized that she had a lot to offer, not just in terms of her intelligence and unique perspective, but also in terms of her empathy and understanding. Caleb was grateful for the friendship they had developed and knew that it would continue to be an important part of his life.

Caleb found himself drawn to Sarah's kindness and her positive energy. He realized that he had been so focused on fitting in with the popular crowd that he had never really taken the time to get to know people like Sarah.

As Caleb and Sarah continued to work on their class project together, their initial collaboration slowly turned into a genuine connection. They started to open up to each other, sharing their thoughts, feelings, and experiences. They discovered that they had more in common than they had initially realized.

As they worked on the project, they found themselves laughing and enjoying each other's company. Caleb began to appreciate Sarah's sense of humor and her ability to see the world in a unique way. He was impressed by how much she had to offer beyond her academic achievements and religious beliefs.

Sarah, in turn, found herself drawn to Caleb's easygoing nature and his willingness to listen to her. She appreciated his interest in learning from her and his openness to new ideas. As they worked on the project, she began to see him as more than just a jock who was focused on sports.

Their shared experience brought them closer together and helped them develop a real connection. They started to spend time together outside of class, going for walks, grabbing a coffee, and enjoying each other's company. As they got to know each other better, they realized that they had formed a strong bond that went beyond their initial collaboration on the project.

By the time their project was complete, Caleb realized that he had developed feelings for Sarah. He wasn't sure if she felt the same way, but he knew that he wanted to spend more time with her, to get to know her better.

Little did he know, their partnership on that class project was just the beginning of a beautiful journey that would change both of their lives forever.

4

Sarah's Dream

***

Caleb learns about Sarah's love for music and her dream of becoming a professional musician, but her strict parents disapprove of her pursuing her passion.

***

Caleb and Sarah were enjoying the warm spring breeze in the park after finishing their homework. Caleb was telling Sarah about his latest soccer game when she suddenly interrupted him.

"Can I share something with you?" she asked, nervously biting her lip.

"Of course," Caleb replied, curious.

"I love music," Sarah said softly. "It's always been my passion. I play the piano and sing, and I've been dreaming of becoming a professional musician since I was a little girl."

Caleb was surprised by her revelation. He had never thought of her as a musician, but he could sense the excitement and joy in her voice as she talked about her dream, and he felt a pang of admiration for her.

"That's amazing, Sarah," he said, smiling. "I had no idea. You should definitely pursue your dream."

Sarah's face fell. "I wish it were that easy," she said, sighing. "My parents don't approve of me pursuing music. They think it's a waste of time and that I should focus on my studies instead."

Caleb felt a twinge of anger on Sarah's behalf. He couldn't imagine having his dreams crushed like that, especially by the people who were supposed to love and support him.

"That's not fair," he said firmly. "You should be able to do what makes you happy. Maybe we can find a way to convince your parents to change their minds."

Sarah shook her head sadly. "It's not that simple. My parents are very strict. They have certain expectations for me, and they don't want me to deviate from them."

Caleb could see the disappointment in her eyes, and he wished he could do something to help her. He knew how important it was to have a dream and to pursue it with passion and determination.

"Have you tried talking to them about it?" Caleb asked, trying to be helpful.

Sarah nodded. "I have, but they just won't listen. They think music is a hobby, not a career."

"Well, I don't think that's true," Caleb said, trying to cheer her up. "Music is a valid career, and if it's something you're passionate about, you should pursue it."

Sarah smiled weakly. "Thanks, Caleb. It means a lot to have someone believe in me."

"Of course," Caleb said, smiling back. "I'll always believe in you."

Over the next few weeks, Caleb and Sarah talked more about her love for music and her struggles with her parents. Caleb listened patiently, offering his support and encouragement. He knew that he couldn't solve all of Sarah's problems, but he wanted her to know that he was there for her, no matter what.

"I wish my parents could see how much music means to me," Sarah said, one day. "It's not just a hobby, it's my life."

"I understand," Caleb said. "Have you thought about maybe showing them how serious you are about music? Like, performing for them or showing them your compositions?"

"I've tried," Sarah said, shaking her head. "But they just don't take me seriously. To them, music is just a distraction from my studies."

Caleb felt a pang of frustration on Sarah's behalf. "That's not fair," he said. "Maybe we could find a way to show them how much music means to you, how it's not just a distraction, but something that brings you joy and fulfillment."

Sarah looked at him with a glimmer of hope in her eyes. "Do you really think we could do that?"

"Absolutely," Caleb said, smiling. "I'm with you every step of the way."

They spent the next few days brainstorming ideas for how to show Sarah's parents how serious

5

Discovering A Shared Love Of Music

* * *

Caleb and Sarah go on their first date to a local music festival and discover a shared love of folk music.

* * *

Caleb and Sarah had been spending more and more time together, and Caleb realized that he was falling in love with her. He knew that he wanted to take their relationship to the next level and ask her out on a real date.

One day, as they were walking home from school, Caleb mustered up the courage to pop the question.

"Sarah, would you like to go on a date with me?" he asked, his heart racing.

Sarah looked up at him, surprised but pleased. "Sure, Caleb," she said, smiling. "What did you have in mind?"

Caleb thought for a moment before an idea struck him. "There's a local music festival happening this weekend," he said. "I thought we could go together and check it out."

Sarah's eyes lit up. "That sounds like fun," she said eagerly.

On the day of the festival, Caleb picked Sarah up at her house. She looked beautiful in a flowing sundress and a wide-brimmed hat, and Caleb felt his heart skip a beat.

"You look amazing, Sarah," Caleb said, smiling.

"Thank you," Sarah replied, blushing slightly. "You look pretty handsome yourself."

Caleb grinned. "Well, I try."

As they made their way to the festival, they talked about their favorite music and their plans for the summer. Sarah was excited to see some of the local bands and to try the different foods and drinks that the festival had to offer.

When they arrived, they were greeted by the sounds of live music and the smells of sizzling food. Sarah's eyes widened as she took in the colorful sights and sounds around her.

"I can't believe I've never been to this festival before," she said, grinning.

Caleb chuckled. "It's one of the best events of the year. I'm glad you're enjoying it."

As they wandered around, they came across a small stage where a young woman was playing guitar and singing. Her voice was sweet and soulful, and Sarah found herself drawn to the music.

"She's really good," she said, nodding her head to the beat.

Caleb agreed. "Yeah, she is. You know, you're pretty good yourself, Sarah. Have you thought about performing at a place like this?"

Sarah's face fell. "I don't think my parents would let me. They don't believe that music is a worthwhile pursuit."

Caleb frowned. "That's not right. You should be able to pursue your dreams, no matter what they are."

Sarah sighed. "I know, but it's not that simple. They have certain expectations for me, and they don't want me to disappoint them."

As they walked through the crowds, Caleb noticed that Sarah's face lit up whenever she heard the sound of a guitar or a fiddle. He took her hand and led her over to a small stage where a group of musicians were playing folk music.

As they listened to the music, Caleb and Sarah discovered that they both shared a love of folk music. They sang along to the lyrics, swaying to the beat, and laughing as they stumbled over the words.

As the sun began to set, Caleb bought them both a pair of ice cream cones, and they sat down on a bench, enjoying the sweet treat and the warm breeze.

"This is perfect," Sarah said, looking up at Caleb with a smile.

Caleb leaned over and kissed her gently on the cheek. "I'm glad you think so," he said, feeling his heart swell with happiness.

As they walked back to Sarah's house, hand in hand, Caleb knew that he had found something special with Sarah. He couldn't wait to see what the future held for them.

6

Hesitation To Commit

***

Caleb starts to fall in love with Sarah, but is hesitant to commit to a serious relationship.

***

As Caleb and Sarah spent more time together, Caleb found himself falling more deeply in love with her. He loved her kind heart, her intelligence, and her passion for music. However, he also felt a nagging sense of hesitation.

Caleb was a popular athlete in high school and had always enjoyed the attention of girls. He wasn't used to committing to a serious relationship, and he worried that he wasn't ready for the kind of commitment that Sarah deserved.

He tried to ignore his feelings and focus on enjoying their time together, but he couldn't shake the sense of unease that lingered in the back of his mind.

One day, as they were walking home from school, Sarah turned to him and asked, "Caleb, is everything okay? You seem a little distant lately."

Caleb hesitated before finally admitting the truth. "I'm just feeling a little unsure about things," he said, his voice low.

Sarah looked at him, her eyes filled with concern. "What do you mean?" she asked.

Caleb took a deep breath before continuing. "I really like you, Sarah," he said. "But I'm just not sure if I'm ready for a serious relationship. I don't want to hurt you."

Sarah's expression softened, and she took his hand in hers. "I appreciate your honesty, Caleb," she said. "But I want you to know that I'm not looking for anything too serious right now either. I just want to enjoy our time together and see where things go."

Caleb felt a sense of relief wash over him. He was grateful for Sarah's understanding and willingness to take things slow.

He smiled at her, feeling more at ease than he had in days. "Thank you, Sarah. I feel the same way," he said. "I think it's important that we both take things one step at a time and enjoy each other's company without any pressure or expectations."

Sarah nodded, still holding onto his hand. "Exactly. I think we'll have a lot of fun together, Caleb," she said, her eyes sparkling with excitement. "And who knows, maybe things will develop into something more serious down the line. But for now, let's just enjoy the moment."

Caleb squeezed her hand gently, feeling a sense of happiness and contentment. He knew that he had made the right decision in being honest with Sarah about his feelings, and he was excited to see where their relationship would take them.

Over the next few weeks, Caleb and Sarah continued to spend time together, enjoying each other's company without any pressure or expectations. Caleb found himself becoming more and more comfortable with the idea of a serious relationship, and he knew that he was falling deeper in love with Sarah every day.

7

Friends' Teasing

***

Caleb's friends tease him about his growing feelings for Sarah, but he begins to ignore their taunts.

***

Caleb's feelings for Sarah were becoming more and more obvious to those around him. His friends, in particular, had begun to take notice of his growing affection for her. They started to tease him about his newfound softness, which made him feel uncomfortable.

The jokes about Caleb being "whipped" and a "puppy dog" around Sarah were constant, and they made him feel even more self-conscious. Caleb didn't know how to respond to his friends' teasing, and he started to worry that they were making fun of him behind his back.

Despite this, Caleb couldn't deny how much he cared about Sarah. He enjoyed spending time with her, and she made him feel happy in a way that no one else had before. However, he was also starting to feel conflicted because of his friends' comments.

Caleb knew that he needed to confront his friends about their teasing, but he didn't want to risk losing their friendship. He also didn't want to make Sarah feel uncomfortable by drawing attention to their relationship. It was a difficult situation, and Caleb wasn't sure how to handle it.

At first, Caleb tried to brush off their comments, but as they continued to escalate, he found himself growing more and more frustrated. He didn't understand why his friends couldn't see how amazing Sarah was and why he was lucky to have her in his life.

One day, as they were hanging out at a local burger joint, Caleb's friend Jake made a particularly crude joke about Sarah, and Caleb snapped.

"Stop it, Jake," he said, his voice low and angry. "Sarah is an amazing person, and I'm lucky to have her in my life. I'm not going to stand here and listen to you guys disrespect her like that."

His friends looked taken aback by his outburst, but Caleb didn't back down. He knew that he needed to stand up for Sarah and for his own feelings.

From that day forward, Caleb's friends were a little more cautious about teasing him about Sarah. Caleb didn't care, though. He knew that his feelings for her were real and important, and he wasn't going to let anyone make him feel ashamed for caring about someone so deeply.

As Caleb continued to spend time with Sarah, he felt himself growing more and more confident in his love for her. He knew that he wanted to be with her, no matter what anyone else thought.

8

Sarah's Faith

***

Sarah invites Caleb to attend her church and he starts to see the depth of her faith and character.

***

Sarah had mentioned her faith to Caleb before, but he had never really understood just how important it was to her until she invited him to attend her church one Sunday. Caleb had always been respectful of Sarah's beliefs, but he had never taken the time to fully grasp their significance in her life.

When Sarah extended the invitation, Caleb was hesitant at first. He had never been particularly religious and wasn't sure what to expect. He wondered if he would feel out of place or if he would be uncomfortable. However, he wanted to support Sarah and show her that he was interested in all aspects of her life.

After some thought, Caleb decided to accept the invitation. He realized that attending Sarah's church would provide him with an opportunity to learn more about her and her faith. He wanted to see what made her so passionate and committed to her beliefs.

As the day approached, Caleb felt a mix of excitement and nerves. He wasn't sure what to wear or what the service would entail. However, he knew that he was doing something meaningful for Sarah, and that made him feel good.

As Caleb and Sarah walked into the small church, Caleb was immediately struck by the sense of community and warmth that filled the space. The members of the congregation greeted them with open arms, and Caleb could feel the genuine kindness and hospitality in their welcomes.

As they made their way to their seats, Caleb noticed how many people came up to Sarah to say hello and exchange hugs. It was clear that she was well-loved and respected by the members of the church. Caleb felt a sense of gratitude and admiration towards Sarah, seeing her in a new light as he witnessed her connections with the people in her community.

The service itself was unlike anything Caleb had ever experienced. The music was uplifting and joyful, and the message from the pastor was filled with hope and encouragement. Caleb found himself drawn in by the sense of peace and comfort that seemed to permeate the room.

By the end of the service, Caleb knew that he had made the right decision in agreeing to come with Sarah. He had witnessed firsthand the love and support that Sarah's church provided, and he could see how important it was to her. He felt grateful for the experience and was eager to learn more about Sarah's faith and her community.

As they left the church, Sarah turned to Caleb with a smile. "What did you think?" she asked.

Caleb hesitated for a moment before answering. "It was really... nice," he said, struggling to find the right words. "I never realized how much your faith means to you. It's... inspiring."

Sarah smiled at him, her eyes shining with gratitude. "It's a big part of who I am," she said. "And I'm glad you got to see that side of me."

As Caleb and Sarah walked home, Caleb felt a newfound sense of respect and admiration for her. He couldn't believe how much he had learned about her in just a few hours. He realized that her faith wasn't just a set of beliefs, but it was a core part of her character and who she was as a person.

Caleb had always known that Sarah was special, but now he saw her in a completely different light. He admired her for her devotion to her faith and her community, and he felt grateful for the opportunity to be a part of it, even if only as an observer.

As they talked about the service and the things that had touched them both, Caleb felt a growing sense of connection with Sarah. He could see that there was so much more to her than he had initially realized, and he was eager to learn more about her and her faith.

He knew that they still had a lot to learn about each other, but he was excited to continue exploring this new side of Sarah and seeing where it might lead them. He felt a sense of openness and curiosity towards her and her beliefs, and he knew that this was just the beginning of a new chapter in their relationship.

9

Parents' disapproval

***

Caleb's parents disapprove of his relationship with Sarah and pressure him to break things off.

***

Caleb sat nervously across from his parents, knowing that the conversation they were about to have was going to be difficult. He had recently started dating Sarah, a girl he had met in his history class, and he was excited about their future together. However, he also knew that his parents were less than thrilled about his new relationship.

As soon as the topic of Sarah came up, Caleb's parents' expressions turned serious. They began to voice their concerns about Sarah's strict religious upbringing, and how they felt it didn't align with their family's values and priorities.

They questioned whether Sarah was a good influence on Caleb and whether she would hold him back from pursuing his goals.. They encouraged him to break things off and focus on more "practical" pursuits, like his athletics and college applications.

At first, Caleb tried to defend his relationship with Sarah, explaining how much she meant to him and how he admired her strength of character and faith. But his parents were unyielding, and as the weeks went on, their pressure began to wear on him.

Caleb was left feeling torn and conflicted after his conversation with his parents. On one hand, he knew that they only wanted what was best for him and had his best interests at heart. But on the other hand, he couldn't imagine his life without Sarah.

He spent hours thinking about what his parents had said and weighing his options. He considered breaking things off with Sarah to please his parents, but the thought of losing her was too painful to bear. He also thought about trying to convince his parents to give Sarah a chance, but he wasn't sure if that was even possible.

As the days went on, Caleb found himself increasingly anxious and stressed. He didn't know how to move forward or what to do next. He felt like he was stuck in a painful internal struggle, pulled in different directions by his love for Sarah and his desire to please his parents.

Finally, he decided to talk to Sarah about it. He couldn't keep this internal struggle bottled up any longer, and he knew that she deserved to know the truth about how he was feeling.

When he broached the subject with her, Sarah listened patiently, her eyes full of understanding and empathy. She didn't try to pressure him into making any particular decision, but simply encouraged him to follow his heart and do what felt right to him..

Over the course of several conversations with Sarah, Caleb slowly came to realize that he needed to follow his heart and stay true to his feelings for her. He knew that his parents' opinions were important to him, but he also knew that he couldn't sacrifice his own happiness for their approval.

Caleb left their conversation feeling a little more at peace, but still unsure of what his next move should be. He knew that he needed to make a decision soon, though, before the tension between him and his parents grew even more unbearable.

10

Falling Out

***

Caleb and Sarah have a falling out after he fails to defend her against a group of bullies at school.

***

Caleb and Sarah were walking through the crowded school hallway when a group of bullies appeared out of nowhere. They started making fun of Sarah's religious beliefs, taunting her about her faith and mocking her for her beliefs.

Caleb was taken aback by their cruel words and was unsure of how to react. He had never been in a situation like this before and didn't want to make things worse for Sarah. He looked over at her, hoping to see some indication of what she wanted him to do.

Sarah's face was flushed with embarrassment and hurt, but she didn't say anything in response to the bullies' taunts. She simply looked down at her feet, trying to ignore their hurtful words.

Caleb felt a pang of guilt in his stomach as he realized that he was just standing there, doing nothing to defend Sarah. He knew that he needed to say something, but he was afraid of making things worse

As they walked away from the bullies, Sarah's disappointment was palpable. Caleb could see the hurt in her eyes and knew that he had let her down. He felt terrible for not standing up for her, especially after all the times she had supported him.

Caleb knew that he needed to make things right with Sarah. He couldn't bear the thought of losing her or damaging their relationship over his inaction. He took a deep breath and gathered the courage to speak to her.

"I'm sorry, Sarah," Caleb said, his voice soft and apologetic. "I should have stood up for you. I don't know why I froze like that. I promise it won't happen again."

Sarah looked at Caleb with a mix of sadness and forgiveness. "I know you didn't mean to hurt me," she said. "But it still hurts that you didn't do anything. I need to know that you have my back, Caleb. I need to know that you'll always be there for me."

Later that day, when Caleb tried to talk to Sarah about what had happened, she was distant and cold towards him. She told him that she needed time to think and left him alone in the hallway.

For the next few days, Caleb tried to reach out to Sarah, but she wouldn't respond to his messages or calls. He began to realize just how much he had hurt her and how much he had taken her for granted. He felt ashamed of his behavior and wished that he could turn back the clock and make things right.

It wasn't until a few weeks later, when Caleb saw Sarah performing at a local coffeehouse, that he was finally able to approach her and apologize for what he had done. He told her how much he cared about her and how sorry he was for not standing up for her when she needed him most.

Sarah was still hurt, but she could see the sincerity in Caleb's eyes. She forgave him, but she made it clear that he would need to earn back her trust if they were going to continue their relationship.

Caleb knew that he had a lot of work to do, but he was willing to do whatever it took to make things right with Sarah. He had realized just how much she meant to him, and he wasn't going to let her go without a fight.

11

Making Amends

***

Caleb realizes how much Sarah means to him and tries to make amends.

***

After the incident with the bullies, Caleb knew that he had to work hard to regain Sarah's trust and prove his love to her. He started by apologizing again, this time in person, and telling her how much he cared about her.

As Caleb immersed himself in Sarah's world, he began to appreciate the beauty and depth of her faith and music. He saw how they brought her joy, comfort, and meaning, and how they helped her navigate life's challenges with grace and resilience.

Attending church with Sarah was particularly eye-opening for Caleb. He was moved by the sense of community and purpose he found there, and he was impressed by the kindness and generosity of the church members. He saw how much Sarah was loved and valued by her church family, and he realized how important they were to her.

Caleb's newfound appreciation for Sarah's faith and music brought them even closer together. They had deep, meaningful conversations about life, love, and spirituality, and they shared their hopes, fears, and dreams with each other. Caleb began to see Sarah not just as his girlfriend, but as his partner and soulmate.

As they spent more time together, Caleb began to realize just how much Sarah meant to him. He saw her kindness, intelligence, and unwavering strength of character, and he knew that he wanted to be a part of her life forever.

Caleb had been struggling with his feelings for Sarah for a long time, but he had never been able to express them fully. One day, he decided that he couldn't keep them bottled up any longer. He knew that he had to take a risk and tell Sarah how he really felt, no matter what the outcome might be.

He asked Sarah to go out to a secluded spot by the lake, where they could talk in private. As they walked along the shoreline, Caleb's heart was pounding with anticipation. He knew that he might be risking their friendship, but he also knew that he couldn't continue to hide his feelings any longer.

Finally, they reached a quiet spot by the water, and Caleb took a deep breath. "Sarah, I need to tell you something," he said, looking into her eyes. "I love you. I've loved you for a long time, and I want to be with you, no matter what. I know that we come from different backgrounds and have different beliefs, but I believe that we can make it work. I just need to know if you feel the same way."

Sarah was taken aback by Caleb's confession. She had always sensed that there was something more between them, but she had never expected him to be so upfront about it. She felt a mix of emotions - surprise, confusion, and a glimmer of hope. She didn't want to get hurt again, but she also didn't want to let go of the possibility of a future with Caleb.

"Caleb, I don't know what to say," she said, her voice shaking slightly. "I care about you a lot, but I've been hurt before, and I don't want to get hurt again. I need to know that you're serious about this, that you're willing to put in the effort to make it work, no matter what obstacles come our way. Can you promise me that?"

As Caleb heard Sarah's words, his heart swelled with joy and relief. He couldn't believe that she had forgiven him and was willing to give their relationship another chance. Overwhelmed with emotion, he looked deeply into her eyes and said, "Sarah, I promise you that I will always take good care of you, fight for you, and be by your side always." He meant every word of it, and he felt a sense of determination and purpose like never before.

As they sat there by the lake, the sun setting behind them, Caleb and Sarah embraced each other in a tender hug. It felt like the weight of the world had been lifted off of their shoulders, and they both knew that they had found something special in each other. Finally, after what felt like an eternity, they shared a sweet and meaningful kiss, sealing their newfound love for each other. Caleb knew that there would be challenges ahead, but he was ready to face them head-on, as long as Sarah was by his side.

12

Reunited

***

Caleb and Sarah reunite and he promises to stand by her side no matter what

***

After their emotional conversation by the lake, Caleb and Sarah's relationship began to flourish once again. Caleb made a conscious effort to be more attentive and caring towards Sarah. He found himself wanting to spend every moment he could with her, and he made sure to show her how much he valued her.

On a peaceful day in the park, Sarah confided in Caleb about the struggles she faced with her family. She spoke about her passion for music and how it was a core part of her identity, but her parents had different ideas for her future. They had always wanted her to pursue a more practical career, one that promised financial stability and job security, like medicine or law. Sarah felt torn between following her dreams and making her parents proud, and it was a source of constant stress and anxiety for her.

Caleb listened intently, and then he made a promise to Sarah. He promised that he would stand by her side, no matter what. He told her that he believed in her talent and her dreams, and he would do everything in his power to help her achieve them.

Sarah was touched by Caleb's unwavering support, and she knew that she could count on him to be there for her through thick and thin. They hugged each other tightly, feeling a deep sense of connection and love.

Caleb's love for Sarah continued to grow stronger each day, and he was determined to be her support system in every way possible. He knew how much her passion for music meant to her, and he was determined to help her achieve her dreams no matter what obstacles they faced.

He spent countless hours practicing with her, providing feedback, and offering encouragement whenever she needed it. He was always by her side, cheering her on, and making sure she knew that he believed in her.

Caleb's unwavering support gave Sarah the courage to pursue her dreams, even when her family didn't understand. She knew that she had someone who loved her for who she was, and that was all the motivation she needed to keep pushing forward.

Together, Caleb and Sarah were a force to be reckoned with. Their love and support for each other only grew stronger with each passing day, and they knew that no matter what challenges came their way, they could overcome them together.

13

Pursuing Sarah's Music Dreams

***

Caleb helps Sarah to secretly pursue her music dreams by recording her songs and uploading them to a popular music-sharing site.

***

Caleb was committed to helping Sarah achieve her dreams of becoming a musician, even if it meant going against her family's wishes. He wanted to find a way to support her without causing any conflict or stress in her family relationships.

One day, Caleb came up with a clever idea. He suggested that they record Sarah's songs and upload them to a popular music-sharing site, but under a pseudonym to keep her identity a secret. This way, Sarah could share her music with the world without fear of her family finding out and causing any conflict.

Sarah was hesitant at first, worried about getting caught and the consequences that might come with it. But Caleb convinced her that it was worth the risk, and that he would be there for her no matter what happened.

They poured their hearts and souls into the project, and Sarah's talent shone through in every note. Caleb spent countless hours helping Sarah record and produce her music, perfecting each song until it was ready to be shared.

They carefully chose a pseudonym that reflected Sarah's unique style and uploaded her songs to the music-sharing site. Within days, her music began to gain popularity, and people all over the world were discovering her talent. Caleb's idea had turned into a great success, and Sarah was thrilled to finally have her music heard.

Sarah was overjoyed by the positive response to her music, and Caleb was proud to have helped her achieve her dream. Even though they couldn't share the success openly, they knew that they had each other's support and love, and that was all that mattered.

14

Parents' Disapproval Of Sarah's Music

* * *

Sarah's music starts to gain traction online, but her parents eventually find out and forbid her from pursuing music further.

* * *

Despite Caleb and Sarah's efforts to keep her music a secret, her songs continued to gain popularity online. People all over the world were touched by her beautiful voice and heartfelt lyrics.

However, their efforts to keep her music a secret were eventually in vain. Sarah's parents found out about her music and were furious. They forbid her from pursuing music any further, citing her obligations to the family and her future prospects.

Sarah was devastated by her parents' reaction. She had finally found something that brought her true joy and fulfillment, and now it was being taken away from her. Caleb felt helpless as he watched Sarah struggle with the weight of her parents' disapproval.

Despite their differences, Caleb and Sarah's families had always gotten along fairly well. Caleb decided to talk to Sarah's parents in an effort to help them understand how much Sarah's music meant to her.

Caleb met with Sarah's parents and tried to explain how much her music meant to her, and how much it meant to the people who listened to it. He told them how much Sarah's talent had grown and how much potential she had as a musician.

However, Sarah's parents remained unmoved. They insisted that she focus on her studies and her future, rather than wasting her time on something as frivolous as music.

Sarah was heartbroken by her parents' reaction, but Caleb remained by her side, offering his love and support. They both knew that Sarah's dreams of becoming a musician were far from over, and they were determined to find a way to make it happen, no matter what it took.

15

Reconciling Dreams And Expectations

***

Caleb and Sarah try to figure out a way to reconcile her music dreams with her parents' expectations.

***

Caleb and Sarah were both determined to find a way to reconcile her music dreams with her parents' expectations. They spent hours brainstorming different ideas and scenarios, hoping to find a solution that would satisfy everyone involved.

One day, Caleb came up with an idea that he thought might work. He suggested that Sarah take part in a talent competition, where she could showcase her music in front of a live audience and potentially gain recognition from music industry professionals.

Sarah was initially hesitant, knowing that her parents would never approve of her participating in such an event. But Caleb was convinced that it was worth a shot. He helped her prepare for the competition, and they practiced day and night, perfecting every note and every word.

As the day of the competition drew closer, Caleb and Sarah could feel the tension mounting. The stakes were high, and they both knew that there was a lot riding on this performance. They had worked tirelessly to prepare for this moment, spending countless hours practicing and perfecting every aspect of the song they had chosen to perform.

But despite their hard work and dedication, there was still a palpable sense of anxiety hanging in the air. Caleb and Sarah were both aware of the risks involved in what they were doing. If Sarah's parents found out about her participation in the competition, it would almost certainly lead to a heated confrontation.

Despite these concerns, however, they were both determined to see it through. They knew that this was a chance for Sarah to shine, to show the world what she was capable of, and to prove to her parents that her music was a talent worth pursuing. So, with their hearts in their throats, they took to the stage and gave it their all.

When the day of the competition arrived, Sarah performed flawlessly. Her voice was pure and angelic, and her original songs touched the hearts of everyone in the audience. Caleb watched from the sidelines, his heart swelling with pride and admiration for the girl he loved.

As Sarah finished her last song, the crowd erupted into thunderous applause. Caleb knew that this was a moment that they would both remember for the rest of their lives. He made his way to the stage, where Sarah was met with a standing ovation from the judges and the audience.

Tears welled up in Sarah's eyes as Caleb took her hand and led her to the front of the stage. He looked at her with so much love in his eyes that Sarah couldn't help but feel overwhelmed. She knew that without Caleb's unwavering support and love, she would have never had the courage to pursue her dreams.

As the judges announced that Sarah had won first place in the competition, Caleb and Sarah embraced each other tightly, tears streaming down their faces. In that moment, they both knew that nothing could ever come between them, not even their families' disapproval.

In the end, Sarah won first place in the competition, and several music industry professionals approached her, expressing interest in working with her in the future. Sarah was overjoyed by her success, but also nervous about how her parents would react.

When she told them about her victory, they were furious at first. But seeing how happy and fulfilled Sarah was, they eventually softened their stance, and agreed to let her continue pursuing music, as long as she also focused on her studies and other obligations.

Caleb and Sarah were thrilled with the outcome, and felt that they had finally found a way to reconcile her music dreams with her parents' expectations. They knew that there would be challenges ahead, but they were determined to face them together, and to never give up on their love or their dreams.

16

Caleb's Injury And Identity Crisis

***

Caleb's athletic career takes a hit after he sustains an injury and he begins to question his identity.

***

Caleb had always been known for his athletic prowess, but one day, his life took an unexpected turn. During a game, he sustained a serious injury that left him with a long and difficult road to recovery. For Caleb, his physical abilities were something he had always taken for granted, never considering a future where they might be taken away. Now, he was forced to reevaluate everything he had ever known about himself, and he was left with a sense of uncertainty about what the future held.

Despite the love and support of his family and friends, Caleb felt like he was a burden to everyone around him. He started to withdraw from his loved ones, feeling ashamed and embarrassed about his injury.

He was also filled with anxiety about the future, worried that he would never be able to play sports again or do the things he enjoyed.

Caleb's recovery was slow and painful, both physically and emotionally. He had to go through a lot of physical therapy, and his progress was often slow and frustrating. But as time went on, he began to slowly regain his strength and mobility. He also began to realize that his injury had given him a new perspective on life, and had taught him to appreciate the things he had taken for granted before.

Sarah's unwavering support and encouragement helped Caleb stay motivated during his recovery. She would visit him regularly and sit by his bedside, chatting with him, playing music, and reading books. She would listen to him talk about his fears and worries, offering comfort and reassurance. Sarah also encouraged Caleb to set small goals for himself, such as taking a few steps or lifting a light weight, and celebrated each achievement with him.

Over time, Caleb began to regain his strength and mobility. With Sarah by his side, he worked hard in physical therapy and gradually started to see progress. He began to realize that his identity was not solely based on his athletic abilities, but on who he was as a person. With Sarah's support, he was able to rediscover his passions and find new ways to pursue them.

Caleb never forgot the impact that Sarah had on his life during that difficult time. He realized that her love and support were the things that truly mattered in life, and he made a vow to always be there for her, just as she had been there for him.

As Caleb slowly began to heal, he started to realize that his identity was not just defined by his athletic abilities. He had other talents and passions, like his love for photography and his interest in history. With Sarah's help and support, Caleb started to explore these other facets of himself, discovering new things about himself and his place in the world.

Eventually, with Sarah's support and encouragement, Caleb was able to make a full recovery and return to the field. However, his experience had left a lasting impression on him. He now saw that there was more to life than just sports and physical abilities.

Caleb began to explore other passions and interests, such as music and writing, which he had previously overlooked. He also made a conscious effort to prioritize his relationships and spend more time with the people who mattered most to him, including Sarah.

Through this process of self-discovery, Caleb realized that his identity was not solely defined by his physical abilities or achievements. Instead, he saw himself as a complex individual with a variety of interests, passions, and relationships. This newfound perspective gave him a greater sense of fulfillment and purpose than he had ever experienced before.

Caleb was grateful for Sarah's unwavering support during his darkest moments and was committed to being there for her in the same way. He understood the importance of human connections and personal growth and was determined to prioritize those things above all else.

Through his injury and recovery, Caleb learned an important lesson about resilience and self-discovery. He knew that there would be more challenges ahead, but he felt better equipped to face them, knowing that he was more than just an athlete, but a complex and multifaceted person with a lot to offer the world.

17

Sarah's Illness

***

Sarah's health takes a turn for the worse and she is diagnosed with a serious illness.

***

Caleb's newfound perspective on life was put to the test when Sarah's health took a sudden turn for the worse. After months of feeling tired and weak, Sarah was diagnosed with a serious illness that left her bedridden and unable to attend school.

Caleb was devastated by the news, feeling powerless and scared for Sarah's well-being. He spent every moment he could at her side, bringing her books, music, and anything else that might help lift her spirits.

Despite the fear and uncertainty that came with Sarah's worsening condition, Caleb remained steadfast in his commitment to her. He spent long hours at the hospital, reading to her, singing to her, and just being there to comfort her. He researched every possible treatment option and spoke with doctors and specialists to ensure that Sarah was receiving the best possible care.

As Sarah's illness progressed, Caleb found himself facing new challenges every day. But he refused to give up hope, even when the odds seemed insurmountable. He drew strength from Sarah's bravery and determination, and he was inspired by the love and support that they shared.

Caleb also began to appreciate the small moments of joy that they shared together. He would bring Sarah her favorite foods, play her favorite movies, and spend hours talking and reminiscing about their shared experiences. In these moments, Caleb realized that love was not about grand gestures or big moments, but about the everyday acts of kindness and compassion that brought them closer together.

Despite the pain and heartache that came with Sarah's illness, Caleb never wavered in his devotion to her. He knew that his love for her was the one constant in an ever-changing world, and he was grateful for every moment they shared together.

At times, Caleb felt overwhelmed by the weight of his responsibilities. Caleb's journey with Sarah taught him the importance of resilience and selflessness. He learned to put his own struggles aside and focus on helping someone else, which gave him a newfound sense of purpose and fulfillment. Though there were moments of doubt and fear, Caleb never gave up on Sarah, and she never gave up on him. Together, they faced each obstacle with determination and hope, and in doing so, they strengthened their bond and deepened their love for each other.

Caleb and Sarah spent countless hours talking about their hopes and dreams for the future, even in the face of Sarah's illness. They would sit in the hospital room, holding hands, and talk about what they wanted to achieve in life.

Sarah would often say, "I don't want to waste any more time. I want to see the world, experience new things, and live life to the fullest."

Caleb would reply, "I'm with you on that. I want to make the most of every moment we have together. And even if things don't go as planned, I'll always be here to support you."

They would talk about their dreams of traveling to exotic places, trying new foods, and meeting interesting people. They talked about starting a family and growing old together.

Sarah would sometimes express her fears, saying, "I don't want to leave you alone, Caleb. I don't want you to have to go through this alone."

Caleb would reassure her, saying, "You won't be alone, Sarah. I'll always carry you with me. And no matter what happens, we'll always have these moments together. They'll be with me forever."

Their conversations were filled with love, hope, and a deep appreciation for the time they had together. Even in the face of uncertainty and fear, they found comfort and joy in each other's company..

Through it all, Caleb learned the true meaning of love and selflessness. He realized that life was precious and fragile, and that the only thing that truly mattered was the people you loved and the memories you made together.

18

Caregiving And Sacrifice

***

Caleb becomes Sarah's primary caregiver and learns the true meaning of love and sacrifice.

***

As Sarah's condition worsened, Caleb became her primary caregiver. He spent long hours at the hospital, taking care of her every need and making sure she was as comfortable as possible. He learned how to administer medication, change dressings, and provide emotional support to Sarah and her family.

Despite the challenges, Caleb remained dedicated to Sarah's care. He understood how important it was for her to have someone by her side, especially during the difficult moments. And so he never wavered in his commitment to her, even as the days turned into weeks and the weeks turned into months.

During this time, Sarah and Caleb's conversations became even more meaningful. They talked about everything from their childhoods to their deepest fears and hopes for the future. Sarah opened up about her fears of dying and leaving behind her loved ones, while Caleb shared his own struggles with finding his purpose in life.

But through it all, they never lost sight of the present moment. They cherished each day they had together, finding joy in the small things like watching the sunrise from the hospital window or sharing a cup of tea.

One day, as they sat together in Sarah's hospital room, Sarah turned to Caleb and said, "Do you ever think about what our lives would be like if things were different?"

Caleb looked at her, unsure of what she meant. "What do you mean?" he asked.

"I mean, if I weren't sick," Sarah said. "If we could just live our lives like any other couple, without all of this...pain."

Caleb felt a lump form in his throat as he thought about what Sarah was saying. He knew that her illness had brought them closer together, but he also knew that it was taking a toll on both of them.

"I do think about it sometimes," Caleb admitted. "But then I remember that every moment we have together is a gift, and I wouldn't trade that for anything."

Sarah smiled, her eyes shining with tears. "You're right," she said. "Every moment we have together is a gift."

And with that, they settled back into their comfortable silence, content in the knowledge that they had each other, no matter what the future held.

Caleb was overwhelmed by the responsibility of caring for someone so sick, but he was determined to do everything in his power to make Sarah's life as comfortable and joyful as possible. He spent his days researching new treatments and therapies that might help her condition, and his nights by her side, reading her favorite books and playing her favorite music.

As Caleb devoted more and more of his time to caring for Sarah, he began to see the true meaning of love and sacrifice. He realized that love was not just a feeling, but an action - a daily commitment to putting someone else's needs before your own.

Through his care for Sarah, Caleb also learned to let go of his own insecurities and fears. He had always defined himself by his athletic prowess, but now he saw that there was so much more to life than just sports. He found fulfillment in caring for Sarah and in the knowledge that he was making a real difference in her life.

In the quiet moments between doctor's appointments and treatments, Caleb and Sarah talked about their dreams for the future. They knew that their time together might be limited, but they remained hopeful and grateful for each day they had.

Caleb and Sarah's conversations during this time often centered on their hopes and dreams for the future, even as they faced the possibility that Sarah's illness might take her life.

One day, as they sat in the hospital room, Sarah spoke softly. "Caleb, I know that we don't have forever together, but I want you to promise me something."

"Anything," Caleb replied, taking her hand in his.

"I want you to promise me that you'll keep chasing your dreams, even after I'm gone. I don't want you to feel like you have to give up on your own goals because of me."

Caleb felt a lump form in his throat. "I promise, Sarah. I'll never forget you or the love we shared, but I'll also keep moving forward, doing everything I can to make the most of my life."

Sarah smiled weakly. "That's all I could ever ask for."

In the days and weeks that followed, Caleb remained by Sarah's side, cherishing every moment they had together. They talked about everything from their favorite memories to their deepest fears, finding solace in each other's presence.

As Sarah's condition worsened, Caleb knew that their time together was running out. But even as he grieved the loss that was to come, he found comfort in the knowledge that he had been there for her when she needed him most.

As the weeks turned into months, Caleb's love for Sarah only grew stronger. He knew that he would do anything for her, no matter the cost.

19

Marriage

***

Caleb and Sarah get married in a small ceremony surrounded by friends and family.

***

Despite the challenges they faced, Caleb and Sarah's love continued to grow stronger. As Sarah's health improved, they began to dream of a future together.

As Sarah's health declined, Caleb knew that he wanted to spend the rest of his life with her. So, one day, he surprised her with a heartfelt proposal in the hospital room they had grown so familiar with. Sarah was thrilled, and they immediately began planning an intimate wedding with their closest loved ones.

But not everyone was on board with their plans. Sarah's parents were still skeptical of Caleb, and they initially opposed the idea of the two getting married. However, Caleb and Sarah were determined to start their lives together, and they persisted. They eventually found a pastor who was willing to marry them, and they exchanged vows in a breathtaking outdoor ceremony surrounded by their family and friends.

They stood together, hand in hand, Caleb and Sarah knew that they were meant to be together, come what may. They were committed to facing whatever challenges came their way, with love and support as their guiding lights.

As they exchanged rings and shared their first kiss as husband and wife, Caleb and Sarah felt a sense of joy and peace that they had never experienced before. They knew that their journey ahead would not be easy, but they were ready to face whatever challenges came their way together.

After the ceremony, they enjoyed a simple reception filled with music, laughter, and love. Caleb watched as Sarah's eyes sparkled with happiness, and he knew that he had made the right choice in marrying her.

As the night wore on, Caleb and Sarah stole away to a quiet corner of the garden. They sat together, holding hands and watching the stars, lost in their own world of love and possibility.

For Caleb, it was a moment he would never forget. He knew that he had found the person he wanted to spend the rest of his life with, and he felt grateful and blessed to have her by his side.

Caleb turned to Sarah and said, "You know, I never thought I'd find someone who truly understood me until I met you."

Sarah smiled and squeezed his hand. "You don't give yourself enough credit, Caleb. You've always had a kind and caring heart. It just took the right person to bring it out."

Caleb leaned in to kiss her, feeling a sense of contentment wash over him. "I don't know what the future holds for us, Sarah, but I know that I want to face it with you by my side."

Sarah nodded, tears of joy in her eyes. "I feel the same way, Caleb. Together, we can overcome anything."

20

Declining Health

***

Sarah's health continues to decline and Caleb struggles with the inevitability of her passing

***

As much as Caleb and Sarah tried to enjoy their time together after their wedding, the reality of Sarah's illness remained a constant presence in their lives. Despite her determination and the best medical care available, her health continued to decline.

Caleb felt helpless as he watched the person he loved most in the world suffer. He struggled to reconcile his faith with the fact that Sarah's condition was not improving, and he felt angry at the unfairness of it all.

As the days passed, Sarah's condition worsened, and Caleb began to fear the worst. He tried to stay positive and hopeful, but the reality of the situation was hard to ignore.

One night, as he sat by Sarah's bedside, he felt overwhelmed with sadness and despair. He knew that he couldn't bear to lose her, but he also knew that he couldn't keep her with him forever.

In the quiet of the hospital room, Caleb sat beside Sarah's bed, holding her hand and feeling the weight of his emotions bearing down on him. He couldn't imagine life without her, and the thought of losing her was almost too much to bear.

Feeling lost and overwhelmed, Caleb turned to prayer. He closed his eyes and spoke to a higher power, asking for the strength and guidance to get through this difficult time. He prayed for the courage to face whatever lay ahead and to support Sarah through her final days.

As he prayed, Caleb felt a sense of peace wash over him. He knew that the road ahead would not be easy, but he also knew that he was not alone. He drew comfort from his faith and from the knowledge that he had loved Sarah with his whole heart and done everything in his power to make her feel cherished and supported.

In the days that followed, Caleb remained by Sarah's side, comforting her and cherishing every moment they had together. They talked about their hopes and dreams, and reminisced about the memories they had shared.

Despite the sadness that surrounded them, they also found moments of joy and laughter. They knew that their love for each other would never fade, even after Sarah was gone.

As Sarah's condition worsened, Caleb found solace in his faith and in the love of their family and friends. He knew that he would miss her terribly, but he also knew that she would always be with him, guiding him and watching over him from above.

21

Sarah's Passing

***

Sarah passes away, leaving Caleb to grapple with his grief and the question of how to move forward.

***

Caleb's heart shattered into a million pieces when Sarah passed away. He couldn't bear the thought of living without her, and every day seemed to be a struggle to find a reason to go on. He was overcome with a deep sense of sadness that permeated every aspect of his life, and he found himself unable to function in the same way he had before. The world seemed to be a dark and unforgiving place, and nothing could bring him comfort or solace. Caleb was left feeling utterly alone, with no idea how to move forward.

Caleb was in a state of shock and disbelief after Sarah's passing. It was as though his world had come to a standstill, and he struggled to find the motivation to do anything. He found himself going through the motions of life, but with no real sense of purpose or direction.

Every task felt pointless, and he found himself withdrawing from his friends and family. Even when they offered him their love and support, he felt isolated and alone in his grief. He couldn't shake the feeling that a part of him was missing, that Sarah was still out there somewhere, just beyond his reach.

In the midst of all this pain, Caleb tried to hold on to the memories he had of Sarah. He would replay their moments together in his mind, trying to recapture the joy and happiness they had shared. But even these memories felt bittersweet, reminding him of what he had lost.

As the days turned into weeks, Caleb slowly began to realize that he couldn't stay stuck in his grief forever. He knew that Sarah would want him to move on with his life, to find new purpose and meaning in her memory. But it was a slow and painful process, and one that he knew would take time.

Still, he held on to the hope that one day, he would be able to find peace and acceptance in his heart. He knew that Sarah would always be a part of him, and that her love would continue to guide him even in her absence.

As he looked back on their time together, he realized how much Sarah had changed him. She had shown him the true meaning of love, and had taught him to value the things that truly mattered in life.

In the midst of his grief, Caleb began to think about hCaleb was in a state of shock and disbelief after Sarah's passing. It was as though his world had come to a standstill, and he struggled to find the motivation to do anything. He found himself going through the motions of life, but with no real sense of purpose or direction.

Every task felt pointless, and he found himself withdrawing from his friends and family. Even when they offered him their love and support, he felt isolated and alone in his grief. He couldn't shake the feeling that a part of him was missing, that Sarah was still out there somewhere, just beyond his reach.

In the midst of his unbearable pain, Caleb held on tightly to the memories he had of Sarah. He often replayed moments of their time together in his mind, trying to recapture the joy and happiness they had shared. But even these memories, which had once brought him so much comfort, now felt bittersweet, only reminding him of what he had lost.

With each passing day, Caleb tried to make sense of his grief and find a way to move forward. He knew that Sarah would want him to find new purpose and meaning in her memory, but the road ahead seemed long and daunting. He struggled to find the strength to face each day, but slowly and steadily, he began to take small steps towards healing.

Despite his sorrow, he clung to the belief that someday he would discover inner tranquility and embrace Sarah's love as a guiding light, even though she was no longer with him. He recognized that Sarah would forever remain an integral part of him, and he resolved to create a charitable organization named after her that would support aspiring young musicians in achieving their goals.

The process of creating the foundation gave Caleb a sense of purpose, and helped him to find some meaning in his loss. He knew that Sarah would have been proud of him, and he found comfort in the knowledge that her legacy would live on.

Although he would never forget the pain of losing Sarah, Caleb knew that he had to find a way to move forward. He started to see the world with fresh eyes, recognizing the beauty and joy that still existed in the world around him.

Through the foundation and his continued involvement in music, Caleb was able to keep Sarah's memory alive, and to continue to honor the love they had shared. In doing so, he found a way to turn his grief into something positive, and to embrace the lessons that Sarah had taught him about love, faith, and the power of music to bring people together.

22

Turning To Sarah's Music

***

Caleb turns to Sarah's music for comfort and inspiration and begins to rediscover his own sense of purpose.

***

Caleb spends hours listening to Sarah's music, finding solace and inspiration in the beautiful melodies and lyrics she created. He starts to realize that Sarah's music is not just something that she loved to do, but it was also a reflection of who she was as a person.

Caleb spends hours listening to Sarah's music, reading her lyrics, and watching videos of her performances. He is struck by the honesty and vulnerability in her songs, and he can't help but feel moved by the way she was able to express her emotions through her music.

Through her music, Caleb begins to see Sarah in a new light. He understands that her illness didn't define her, but rather it was just one part of who she was. He sees that she was a strong and passionate person who never gave up on her dreams or her faith, even in the face of immense adversity.

Inspired by Sarah's example, Caleb begins to search for his own sense of purpose. He starts volunteering at the hospital where Sarah received treatment, helping other patients and their families navigate the difficult journey of illness. He also begins to write about his experiences, sharing his story with others and hoping to inspire them in turn.

Slowly but surely, Caleb begins to find meaning and fulfillment in his life again. He knows that he will always carry Sarah with him, but he also understands that she would want him to keep living and growing, to find joy and purpose in each new day.

As Caleb continues to write, he finds that his music becomes a way to connect with others who are also struggling with grief and loss. He performs at local coffee shops and open mic nights, sharing his own story through his music.

Through his performances, Caleb meets others who have also been touched by loss, and he begins to form a community of support and understanding. He realizes that he is not alone in his pain and that his music can be a source of healing for others.

As time goes on, Caleb finds that his music has become more than just a hobby or a creative outlet. It has become a way for him to honor Sarah's memory and to continue the work she began in helping others through their pain.

And in the process, he discovers that his own life has taken on a new sense of purpose and meaning, one that he could never have imagined before Sarah came into his life.

As he spends more time writing and playing music, Caleb begins to feel a sense of peace and clarity that he had never experienced before. He starts to see his life in a new light and realizes that he can still make a difference in the world, even without Sarah by his side.

He also finds support from the community of musicians and music lovers that he meets through his performances. They understand his pain and connect with his music in a way that is both healing and inspiring.

As Caleb continues to share his own music and perform Sarah's songs, he realizes that he has found a new family in the music community. They support him and encourage him to keep creating, and he feels grateful to have found a place where he belongs.

Through his journey of grief and healing, Caleb has discovered the power of music to heal, inspire, and connect people. He knows that Sarah would be proud of the way he has continued to honor her memory and find his own path in life.

23

Pursuing Music Career

***

Caleb decides to pursue a career in music in honor of Sarah and her dreams.

***

Caleb's passion for music continues to grow and he realizes that he wants to make a career out of it. He knows that pursuing music full-time would be a big risk, but he feels a deep sense of purpose in carrying on Sarah's legacy and making her dreams a reality.

Caleb begins to focus more on his music and starts to perform at bigger venues, gaining more recognition and support. He also starts to record his own songs and release them online, building a following and connecting with fans all over the world.

With each new song and performance, Caleb feels Sarah's presence with him, guiding him and inspiring him to pursue his passion with everything he has.

Despite the challenges and obstacles he faces along the way, Caleb never loses sight of his dream. He knows that it won't be easy, but he also knows that he has the talent, the drive, and the love of Sarah to see him through.

With the support of his family and friends, Caleb starts to pursue music more seriously. He begins to write and record his own songs, putting his heart and soul into each one. He plays gigs whenever he can, building up a following and slowly but surely making a name for himself in the local music scene.

Caleb's dedication and talent don't go unnoticed, and he eventually catches the attention of a record label. They offer him a contract, and Caleb is thrilled to have the opportunity to share his music with a wider audience.

As Caleb's career takes off, he never forgets the person who inspired him to pursue music in the first place. He dedicates each performance to Sarah and makes sure that her music is always a part of his setlist.

Through his music, Caleb continues to spread the message of love, faith, and hope that Sarah believed in so strongly. He knows that he couldn't have gotten where he is without her, and he is determined to honor her memory in everything he does.

As Caleb takes the stage, he can feel Sarah's presence with him, guiding him and inspiring him to be the best musician and person he can be. He knows that she would be proud of him, and he is grateful every day for the love and inspiration she brought into his life.

24

Success in music

***

Caleb's music career takes off and he becomes a successful musician, but never forgets the impact that Sarah had on his life.

***

Caleb's music career takes off after he starts performing at local bars and small music festivals. His unique sound and heartfelt lyrics quickly gain him a following, and he soon signs a record deal with a major label.

As Caleb's fame grows, he becomes more and more successful, but he never forgets the impact that Sarah had on his life. He continues to write songs about her, incorporating her love of music and her unwavering faith into his own work.

Despite the success he found through his music, Caleb couldn't shake off the sorrow that lingered in his heart. But Sarah's music continued to be his guiding light, offering him solace and inspiration when he needed it most. In one of her songs, he found these lyrics that spoke to him:

"When the night is dark and long

And you feel like you can't go on
Just close your eyes and hear my song
And know that you're never alone"

As he tours the country, playing sold-out shows and sharing his story with fans, Caleb realizes that his music has become a way to honor Sarah and the love they shared. He knows that she would be proud of him and the impact he's making on the world.

Through his music, Caleb finds a sense of purpose and fulfillment that he never thought possible. He knows that Sarah will always be with him, guiding him on his journey and inspiring him to be the best version of himself.

25

Reflection and remembrance

Caleb reflects on his journey and realizes that Sarah's love and legacy will always be a part of him

As Caleb sits in his dressing room before a big concert, he takes a moment to reflect on his journey. His music career has taken off in ways he never could have imagined, and he's grateful for the success he's achieved. But more than anything, he's grateful for the love and inspiration that Sarah brought into his life.

He thinks about the lyrics of one of his most popular songs, which was inspired by Sarah's unwavering spirit and her love for music:

"Your light shines on, even though you're gone

I hear your voice in every song

Your memory lives on, forever strong

And I know that you're never really gone"

Caleb takes a deep breath, feeling the weight of Sarah's legacy on his shoulders. He knows that he has a responsibility to keep her memory alive through his music, and he's determined to do so with every note he plays.

He thinks back to the day they met in their high school English class, and how dismissive he was of her at first. But as he got to know her, he realized that there was something special about her. Her quiet strength and deep faith had drawn him in, and he couldn't deny the connection they had.

Even after they had their falling out and reconciled, Sarah's illness had been a heavy burden to bear. But Caleb had never given up on her, and he had done everything in his power to make her feel loved and cared for. When she had passed away, he had been devastated, but her memory had inspired him to keep going and pursue his own dreams.

As he reminisces about their time together, a line from one of Sarah's songs comes to mind: "Love is not a feeling, it's a choice we make."

Caleb smiles, knowing that Sarah had lived by those words and had taught him to do the same. He had chosen to love her, and that love had given him the strength to keep going even after she was gone.

Feeling a renewed sense of purpose, Caleb takes a deep breath and heads out to the stage, ready to share his music and Sarah's legacy with the world.

Now, as he takes the stage to the roar of the crowd, Caleb knows that Sarah is with him in spirit. He sings the songs that she had written and recorded, the music that had touched so many hearts and had given her a voice in a world that had tried to silence her. And as he finishes his set and the crowd cheers, he knows that he has honored her memory in the best way possible.

As he leaves the stage and heads back to his dressing room, Caleb knows that Sarah's love and legacy will always be a part of him. He may have started off as a directionless high school athlete, but because of her, he had found his purpose and his passion. And for that, he will always be grateful.

Epilogue

Years later, Caleb has become a successful musician, touring the world and sharing his music with thousands of fans. He continues to honor Sarah's memory by performing her songs and sharing her message of love and faith with audiences everywhere. Caleb has found love again, but Sarah will always hold a special place in his heart. He often reflects on the lessons he learned from Sarah's life and their time together. He knows that she would be proud of the person he has become and the impact that their love and music has had on so many people. As Caleb finishes his latest concert, he looks out at the crowd and thinks of Sarah, grateful for the journey they shared and the legacy they created together.

www.ingramcontent.com/pod-product-compliance
Lightning Source LLC
Chambersburg PA
CBHW041454010526
44107CB00013B/1036